HOW TO TURN YOUR POETRY INTO PROFIT!

BY: JENNIFER BROWN BANKS
FOUNDER OF POETS UNITED TO ADVANCE THE ARTS

MARKET$ & METHODS TO GET PAID NOW

BY: JENNIFER BROWN BANKS
FOUNDER OF POETS UNITED TO ADVANCE THE ARTS

INTRODUCTION

There are many ways to earn an income for today's resourceful writer, particularly in the digital age. In fact, "the starving artist" image is so '80's! Trust me; I should know. In my long and colorful career as a professional scribe, I've pursued darn near all things legal and literary.

In the process, I've discovered that one often overlooked genre for making money is poetry. That's right. Though most of us mere mortals won't reach the "heights" of Elizabeth Barrett-Browning or perform for the president like Maya Angelou, or achieve rock-star status like Amanda Gorman, we can still share our work with broad audiences and be compensated nicely in the process. Hello!

According to a report released by the National Endowment of the Arts, poetry is more popular than ever before. Worth noting here is that "the number of poetry readers in the United States has nearly doubled from 6.7% of American adults in 2012 to nearly 12% in 2017."

Got poetry? Did you know that BookThat Poet.com facilitates paid performances and workshops for poets across the country currently, for those listed in their online directory?
A caveat here: poetry won't likely pay your monthly mortgage, but it can finance food for the cupboard; keep the lights on; or keep your wine stash well-stocked.

HERE ARE 6 AVENUES TO GO FROM PASSION TO PROFIT THIS YEAR:

PUBLIC READINGS

April is officially National Poetry Month. I make it a point to use this special time each year to pitch local libraries, universities and coffee shops to be added to their special events.
The last time I did, I received $200.00 for reading a few pieces at a fun poetry festival. You can too.

OPEN MIC COMPETITIONS

With the popularity of "Spoken Word" and performance poetry, many venues host open mic nights (sometimes along with karaoke). Here's a chance to compete and meet other poets for a modest cash price for the selected evening's winner.

TEACHING WORKSHOPS

Workshops are typically offered at libraries, arts centers, adult continuing education classes, schools, and writing clubs. It's a great opportunity to educate and inspire others who may be interested in learning how to pen poetry, know more about the different styles and forms of poetry, or those who simply enjoy poetry analysis and interpretation. Additionally, poets can present online classes and earn cash

through platforms like TEACHABLE.COM and
UDEMY.COM.

<u>SELLING BOOKS & GIFT ITEMS</u>

Self-published poetry chapbooks and framed gift items can
increase your visibility and your bottom line. They can be
sold at local gift shops, vendors' fairs and even at family
reunions.

<u>CHAPBOOK CONTESTS</u>

There are various publishers and organizations that
compensate poets via competitions for short poetry
collections (usually 20-40 poems) for a potential publishing
contract and cash. PALOOKA PRESS provides an
honorarium of $200.00 and 20 free copies of the winning
author's published book. Visit their site here for more
details:

https://palookamag.submittable.com/submit/144056/palooka
-press-chapbooks

<u>ONLINE MAGAZINES & WEBSITES</u>

Numerous online publications now pay for well-crafted
poetry on selected themes and general topics.
Three Penny Review, for example pays $200.00 per poem.
Not bad for brief work. Wouldn't you agree?

ADDITIONAL STRATEGIES FOR OPTIMAL SUCCESS

1. **KNOW YOUR AUDIENCE.**

Whether submitting poetry to a publication or reading your pieces before a live audience for a fundraiser, it's important to know a little about who they are and the group's collective "leanings." Are they the corporate, conservative type? What's the group's mission or brand? Will there be children in the mix? For example, I would choose different poems to share for my church events than I would for karaoke night audiences.

2. **STUDY THE WORKS OF OTHER TALENTED POETS FROM DIFFERENT ERAS AND WRITING STYLES TO HONE YOUR CRAFT AND CULTIVATE YOUR "VOICE."**

This will broaden your horizons; help you to learn more about various techniques; inform your writing; and enable you to be more diverse in your expression. I read (and listen to) everything from Barrett-Browning, to Angelou, to Frost, to Tupac Shakur. Check out Def Poetry Jam's YouTube channel for pointers. Remember, "verse"-atility allows you to appeal to varied audiences and different demographics.

3. **WHEN THERE IS FINANCIAL COMPENSATION INVOLVED, PROTECT YOURSELF BY HAVING THE SPECIFICS OUTLINED IN A WRITTEN CONTRACT.**

Keep it simple. The agreement doesn't have to be documented with a multi-paged, complicated contract with a bunch of legal jargon; something as basic as a detailed email where both parties mutually agree on said terms will seal the deal.

4. REMEMBER, "PRACTICE MAKES PERFECT."

If you're seeking to be paid for your poetry performances and to be considered a true "professional" your mindset, approach and delivery can make all the difference. Don't just wing it. Whether you are auditioning for a poetry gig, or have already been chosen to perform for an audience, be sure to practice beforehand. Consider rehearsing in front of a mirror at home or recording yourself reading your poems. Doing so will ensure that you are as "polished" and prepared as possible; which increases the likelihood of future bookings and referrals.

IN CONCLUSION…If you've been penning poetry for recreation, it's time for a paradigm shift.

Follow these timely tips to go from recreation to compensation this year!

MARKETS THAT PAY POETS

THREE PENNY REVIEW

https://www.threepennyreview.com/submissions.html

PAYS $200.00 PER ACCEPTED POEM

RATTLE

https://www.rattle.com/submissions/guidelines/

PAYS $200.00 PER POEM

CONFRONTATION MAGAZINE

https://confrontation-magazine.org/submit/

RANGES $75.00-$100.00

CHICAGO WRITERS ASSOCIATION
WRITE CITY MAGAZINE

PAY VARIES BASED UPON MEMBERSHIP STATUS

https://www.chicagowrites.org/write_city_magazine/guidelines

CHICKEN SOUP FOR THE SOUL

https://www.chickensoup.com/story-submissions/possible-book-topics/

THIS POPULAR ANTHOLOGY PAYS $200.00 PER POEM

RUMINATE MAGAZINE

https://www.ruminatemagazine.com/pages/submissions

PAYS $20.00 PER PAGE

MOMENT POETRY

https://www.momentpoetry.com/how-it-works/

PAYS 25% OF PRICE FOR LIMITED EDITION POETRY
INSPIRED ARTWORK
THAT THEY PRODUCE

4 STRATEGIES TO SECURE FUTURE BOOKINGS AND GET PAID

In my long and lovely career as a poet, I have had the pleasure of performing at an array of venues, for an assortment of functions and affairs.
I have read my works at fundraisers; recited poetry at weddings; shared selections from my published books at libraries and schools. I have even done tributes at funerals. Both individually and with my poetry group.

These paid performances and fun opportunities to sell my poetry collections resulted from four main activities.

Here I provide my insider's tips, in no particular order:

1. NETWORKING

Sometimes it's possible to score a booking through folks you know, who may have an interest in your services. For example, I once met a woman online who happened to have been a member of a writer's organization to which I belonged in my local area. Through our group's message board, she was promoting an upcoming arts event (seeking support). Upon reading this, I emailed her directly. I let her know about my work as a poet; exchanged ideas; and later landed a performance at a nice, intimate coffee shop. Pay with this gig was modest, but included free desserts for the night. Sweet indeed!

2. RESEARCHING

Periodically, I check community newspapers and local websites for weekend Calendar of Events. This is how I learn of library workshops, new business openings, writing conferences, etc.
In doing so, I assess whether or not poetry would fit in as a possible entertainment option for the potential audience. If so, I call, email or follow the guidelines provided at the respective site to offer my services to be included in the line-up of events. You should too.

3. PITCHING

Follow strategy # 2. But also consider drafting a pitch letter to be sent out and used as a future template (to be modified) for different events and causes.

4. ADVERTISING

To help to get the word out about my poetry and creative services, I have created a website that showcases my books, sample poems, and my contact information. See below:
https://poetsunitedtoadvancethearts.blogspot.com/

I have also listed my availability at <u>BOOKTHATPOET.COM</u>,
which provides listings for poets across the country.

For optimal results try one or a combination of the above
strategies.

To enhance your efforts, be sure to have professional
business cards created to pass out to family, friends and
neighbors. It works if you work it!

PRO POETS OFFER MORE SUCCESS TIPS FOR 2022....

"Teaching and Judging are some ways to generate income for poetry.

About teaching - You don't need to be a college professor to teach poetry writing - libraries, poetry writing clubs, arts organizations and more often seek poetry writing workshop facilitators. Come up with your own list of workshop ideas that you might lead. Is there a poetic form that you have a strong interest in? Or is there a poetic theme that you think might stimulate the imaginations of a room full of poets? Flesh out your list of ideas with a clever workshop title and a one or two sentence description. Come up with a variety of published example poems to share with workshop participants.

About judging - serve as a judge for a poetry contest. Some organizations will offer an honorarium for your service. Build up your credentials as a dependable judge by initially volunteering to judge a contest."

---JENNIFER DOTSON, FOUNDER OF HIGHLAND PARK POETRY

"Respect your work, time and profession. Then, you'll get paid for doing your poetry. That's what a professional is.

Request 1/2 down for your payment and get the remaining half when you show up to share your poetry. This is how many musicians do it. Know your worth. You must at least get paid for that one gig the amount you'd make in a day at your regular 9-5 job. Usually a professional poet sharing for a day should be paid $250 or more but this is after you've built many literary credentials. Starting out $125 is reasonable for an hour of reading/reciting about 15 to 20 short poems. Then q & a afterwards."

---Henry L. Jones
Inaugural Poet Laureate
Hendersonville, TN

"It may seem elementary, and you've probably heard it before, but when submitting, follow the journal's guidelines. Many have different ones: double spaced or single, a single document for all 10 poems or separate files, bio of xx words, name and address on every page or no name or other ID info anywhere, contribute no more than once a millennium . . . .
Such attention shows you've read the guidelines carefully and followed them, like a true professional, and your entry is likely to be at least read."

---NOELLE STERNE, AUTHOR/NOVELIST/POET

"Want to increase your poetry pay and promote your work? Hire Jennifer! "

--- MARY LAFORGE, AUTHOR/VISUAL ARTIST/POET

"Save your work. Don't throw away anything. Not to encourage hoarding or fire hazards but in this age of computer storage on discs, USBs, and memory cards, you can preserve your work. I've been surprised by unfinished pieces or ideas from years ago I come across, which I then polish, update, and turn into a finished product worthy of submission."

--- G.MERRIWETHER, A.K.A. POET COP

SUBMISSION TRACKER

POEM TITLE	DATE SUBMITTED	NAME OF PUBLICATION	STATUS

ADDITIONAL POETRY RESOURCES & WEBSITES

WRITE BETTER POEMS (TUTORIALS AND TIPS)

https://www.writebetterpoems.com/

NEW PAGES (LISTING OF POETRY CONTESTS AND CALLS FOR SUBMISSIONS)

https://www.newpages.com/classifieds/writing-contests

POETS AND WRITERS (AN ARRAY OF RESOURCES ON CONTESTS & FUNDING)

https://www.pw.org/

TRISH HOPKINSON (POETRY INTERVIEWS AND MARKETS)

https://trishhopkinson.com/2022/03/16/chill-subs-interview-new-site-to-find-the-right-home-for-your-writing/

POETS UNITED TO ADVANCE THE ARTS (ADVOCACY AND HOW-TO ARTICLES)

https://poetsunitedtoadvancethearts.blogspot.com/

ABOUT THE AUTHOR

Jennifer Brown Banks is an award-winning poet, popular blogger and author.
She has published seven books of poetry on varied themes, over the decades.
She is the founder and president of Poets United to Advance the Arts, based in Illinois.

Banks holds a bachelor's degree in Business Management. She formerly served on the Board of Directors of Chicago Writers Association for ten years.

CONTACT INFO:

JENNIFER BROWN BANKS
POETS UNITED
P.O. BOX 437051
CHICAGO, IL 60643

EMAIL: COFFEEJENS@GMAIL.COM

Image credits: Pixabay.com